I0454917

Expeditionary Border Security Operations:
Eliminating the Seams

A Monograph
by
LTC Michael J Zinno
US Army Reserve

MENS EST CLAVIS VICTORIAE

School of Advanced Military Studies
United States Army Command and General Staff College
Fort Leavenworth, Kansas

AY 2008

Approved for Public Release; Distribution is Unlimited

SCHOOL OF ADVANCED MILITARY STUDIES

MONOGRAPH APPROVAL

LTC Michael James Zinno

Title of Monograph: Expeditionary Border Security Operations: Eliminating the Seams

This monograph was defended by the degree candidate on 22 May 2008 and approved by the monograph director and reader named below.

Approved by:

_____   Monograph Director
Jacob Kipp, Ph.D.

_____   Monograph Reader
Richard M Cabrey, COL, FA

_____   Director,
Stefan J. Banach, COL, IN   School of Advanced
                                         Military Studies

_____   Director,
Robert F. Baumann, Ph.D.   Graduate Degree
                                         Programs

Abstract

Expeditionary Border Security Operations: Eliminating the Seams by LTC Michael J Zinno, US Army Reserve, 56 pages.

Within the context of the current US government endeavor to unify its actions and build partner-nation military capabilities in the Global War on Terror (GWOT), this monograph seeks to determine the potential value of utilizing expeditionary interagency border security teams (BSTs) to conduct border security operations and training during theater security cooperation activities. Specifically, this monograph answers whether border security operations will assist nations in countering destabilizing elements within their nations and, subsequently, impacting the operational scope and capability of global terrorist networks that threaten US national security.

This paper uses case studies in the Tri Border area of South America and the Trans Sahel region in Africa to examine the threat from a convergence of terrorist and criminal organizations toward complementary efforts and their use of porous border regions to conduct logistical activities. This convergence greatly expands the scope and capability of each individual terrorist or criminal organization and the cumulative effect can overwhelm the security forces of many nations and provide a critical link in a logistical network tracing a path to the border of the US.

To counter this threat the paper analyzes a case study of Post WW II Germany and develops a framework for border security operations consisting of eight principles: consistent national agreements established upfront between allied and partner nations concerning border security policies; integrated border security policies at the US national level; the ability to communicate with the local populace culturally and linguistically and provide outlets for information requirements from the local population; early intervention to prevent a collapse in security that would require major international military intervention; a border security force which has a static and mobile capability; the use of indigenous population in border security forces; an integrated economic development plan; and a graduated suppression of black market activities.

Adding to this framework the paper analyzed the development of the Israeli Border Police and found a set of principles to aide in future border security operations and training missions. In summary the principles of an effective border security force are; permanent status as government organization under the command and control of the National Police, with a decentralized flexible tactical command structure, that is culturally diverse, integrated into society and specially trained and supervised by a professional cadre of mature NCOs and Officers.and

Utilizing the framework developed from the case studies, the paper investigates existing GWOT border security initiatives in Africa and South America and concludes that these programs have limited effectiveness. The shortfalls in these initiatives lead to five recommendations to increase the impact of these programs on US national security. First, the US should integrate its various national strategies at the NSC level to develop a comprehensive strategy to address the asymmetric threats to US borders. Second, a US joint doctrine publication should be developed to codify the principles of border security operations, force development and training highlighted in the case studies. Third, the US Army and US Marine Corps should develop the capability to train and develop foreign border security forces, facilitate the construction of necessary border security infrastructure, and make these capabilities available to GCCs for use during Theater Security Cooperation Activities. Fourth, develop in all applicable US government agencies a capability to provide a sufficient amount of deployable civilian employees with expertise in border security operations. Finally, as nations develop innovative solutions to counter the adaptive transnational threats, those departments and agencies involved with US border security teams must develop a process for sharing, learning and implementing new changes to stay ahead of the threats' ability to communicate its adaptations.

TABLE OF CONTENTS

FIGURES

ACRONYMS AND ABBREVIATIONS

BORTAC- Border Patrol Tactical Unit

BST- Border Security Team

CATA- Civil Affairs Team Alpha

TPT- Tactical Psychological Operations Team

ISR- Intelligence, Surveillance and Reconnaissance

DEA- Drug Enforcement Agency

SHAEF- Supreme Headquarters Allied Expeditionary Force

COIN- Counterinsurgency

DOA- Department of Agriculture

CBP- Customs and Border Patrol Agency

DOJ- Department of Justice

HLS- Department of Homeland Security

DOS- Department of State

USAID- United States Agency for International Development

CIA- Central Intelligence Agency

DENTCAP- Dental Civic Action Program

MEDCAP- Medical Civic Action Program

VETCAP- Veterinarian Civic Action Program

DIA- Defense Intelligence Agency

IGAD- Inter Governmental Authority on Development

NGIA- National Geospatial Intelligence Agency

USACE- United States Army Corps of Engineers

MNJ- *Mouvement des Nigeriens pour la Justice*

CENTCOM- US Central Command

EUCOM- US European Command

CTC- Crime Terror Continuum

NSTC- National Strategy to Counter Terrorism

GWOT- Global War on Terrorism

ATF- Alcohol, Tobacco and Firearms Agency

FM- Field Manual

DOD- Department of Defense

TBA- Tri Border Area, referring to South America

TSCTI- Trans Sahel Counter Terrorism Initiative

EACTI- East Africa Counter Terrorism Initiative

PSI- Pan Sahel Initiative

TCO- Transnational Criminal Organization

GTN- Global Terrorist Network

GSPC- *Groupe Salafiste pour la Predication et le Combat*

AQIM- Al Qaeda in the land of the Islamic Maghreb

CJTF HOA- Combined Joint Task Force, Horn of Africa

Introduction

Research Question

Within the context of the current US government endeavor to unify its actions and build partner-nation military capabilities in the Global War on Terror (GWOT), this monograph seeks to determine the potential value of utilizing expeditionary interagency border security teams (BSTs) to conduct border security operations and training during theater security cooperation activities. Specifically, this monograph answers whether border security operations will assist nations in countering destabilizing elements within their nations and, subsequently, impacting the operational scope and capability of global terrorist networks that threaten US national security.

Relevance

The threats to the US border since the end of the Cold War have manifested themselves in many forms such as terrorism, pandemic disease, drug trafficking, human smuggling, and transnational criminal activities. In recent years, a dangerous trend called the Crime Terror Continuum has emerged, which indicates that many of the organizations that conduct and support these threat activities are converging their operations. This convergence greatly expands the scope and capability of each individual terrorist or criminal organization and the cumulative effect can overwhelm the security resources of many nations. In places such as the Tri Border area of South America and the Trans Sahel region in Africa, this overwhelming convergence has greatly destabilized these regions. Once destabilized, these regions can provide a critical link in a logistical network for the convergent threat organizations which can trace a path right to the borders of the US.

Background

Border security and illegal immigration along the US/Mexico border dominate many debates in the US Congress. While both sides of the debate argue the positive and negative economic and social impacts of illegal immigration, there appears to be general agreement that potential terrorists illegally entering the US through the Mexican border are a national security concern. Given the fact that these terrorists typically originate from nations other than Mexico, the US southern border is probably the last hurdle in a series of smuggling and staging points originating from a terrorist sanctuary in a lawless area of the world. The magnitude of this threat is large. According to the 2007 House Committee on Homeland Security report, in fiscal year 2006 the US Border Patrol apprehended 108,025 Other Than Mexicans (OTMs) attempting an illegal border crossing. Furthermore, it estimates that those apprehended only represent 10 to 30% of all illegal border crossings.[1] Any one of the OTMs not apprehended, could potentially be a terrorist and this fact is alarming. Addressing this threat to US national security requires a comprehensive strategy from the US government.

Within the context of the US National Strategy for Combating Terrorism (NSCT), the US government border security strategy is the responsibility of the US government lead agency on border security, the US Customs and Border Protection Agency (CBP) of the Department of Homeland Security (DHS). The CBP strategic plan recognizes that waiting until a terrorist threat reaches the US border limits the effectiveness of any strategy. The CBP strategy calls for a defense-in-depth approach and one of its stated strategic objectives is to "push the nation's zone of security beyond physical US borders through partnerships and extended border initiatives to deter and combat the threat of terrorism."[2] The US governments' "Plan Merida," which calls for the US to give Mexico $500 million in aid over the next 12 months "in the form of training for the police and military as well as aircraft and advanced technology at border crossings," is a good

---

[1] Sub Committee on Investigations of House Committee on Homeland Security, "A Line in the Sand: Confronting the Threat at the Southwest Border," under "Vulnerability to Terrorist Infiltration," http://www.house.gov/mccaul/pdf/Investigaions-Border-Report.pdf (accessed on December 15, 2007).

[2] US Customs and Border Protection Agency, "Strategic Plan 2005-2011," under "Preventing Terrorism at Ports of Entry: Strategic Objective 1.4," http://www.cbp.gov/linkhandler/cgov/toolbox/about/mission/strategic_plan_05_11.ctt/strategic_plan_05_1 1.pdf (accessed on November 19, 2007).

example of a border security package needed to partially address the US strategy.[3] However, south of Mexico and in other nations around the globe, the border security needs are equally as pressing, and the Department of Defense is uniquely positioned to take a larger role in facilitating the US border security strategy through its Security Cooperation Activities.

Guatemala, Belize, El Salvador, Honduras, Nicaragua, Costa Rica and Panama are all likely targets for assistance, however; Guatemala may be the best place to start. For example, in the Mexican/Guatemalan border town of Tapachula groups can illegally access a network of freight trains that travel all the way up to the US border creating a "smuggling superhighway" through Mexico. The 600 mile border between Mexico and Guatemala provides ample opportunity for illegal border crossing of people and illicit goods. An International Relations and Security Network 2006 report summed up the problem with the Mexican/Guatemalan border this way, "Guatemala is the acute point where Central America makes the bridge between South American supply and North American demand for illegal drugs. Guatemalans complete the link essential to the drug trade that connects Colombia's cocaine with Mexican buyers."[4] This critical link in the drug trade may also be utilized by other criminal and terrorist organizations. Guatemala is just one example out of many nations where there is opportunity for the US to partner with these nations to improve border security, which if effective will disrupt the transit of people and illicit goods before they reach the US/Mexico border and achieve the CBP strategy.

---

[3] James McKinley Jr, "Bush Asks Congress For $1.4 Billion To Fight Drugs in Mexico," New York Times, October 23, 2007, http://www.nytimes.com/2007/10/23/world/americas/23mexico.html (accessed on November 18, 2007).

[4] Sam Logan, "Guatemala: Possible 'Columbianization," International Relations and Security Network, October 13, 2006, under "News and Current Affairs: Security Watch," http://www.isn.ethz.ch/news/sw/details.cfm?id=16787 (accessed on December 15, 2007).

Interagency Context

The development of the US Global War on Terror strategy in the aftermath of the 9/11 attacks against the US recognized an emerging need for a multidisciplinary approach. Although the military would surely play a large role in the execution of this strategy, it became clear to US government leaders that to defeat fully the adversaries of the US, it must "attack" in the realms of economics, diplomacy and information, with the support of many nations across the globe. The NSCT published in February 2003 summarized these concepts:

> The struggle against international terrorism is different from any other war in our
> history. We will not triumph solely or even primarily through military might.
> We must fight terrorist networks, and all those who support their efforts to spread
> fear around the world, using every instrument of national power-diplomatic,
> economic, law enforcement, financial, information, intelligence, and military.[5]

Many interagency actions have been initiated, but progress in this area has been slow particularly in actions that are of an expeditionary nature. A 2007 report from the Center for Strategic and International Studies reviewed US interagency Counter-Terrorism (CT) programs in Africa and determined that "there is a lack of coherent strategic vision and authoritative plans to guide identification of critical US government CT capabilities, to rationalize resources across agency boundaries, and to integrate activities in target countries."[6]

The US actions in Iraq also typify the challenges of interagency, the expeditionary nature of the US campaign against terrorism, and the need for unified action. Almost four years into the Iraq conflict, Multi-National Force Iraq (MNF-I) Commander General David H. Petraeus describes an unfulfilled unified effort in countering the strong insurgency. He insists that among

---

[5] George Bush, "National Strategy for Combating Terrorism," under "Introduction," http://www.whitehouse.gov/news/releases/2003/02/counter_terrorism/counter_terrorism_strategy.pdf (accessed on October 17, 2007).

[6] J. Stephen Morrison and Kathleen Hicks, "Integrating 21st Century Development and Security Assistance," *Final Report of the Task Force on Non-Traditional Security Assistance, Center for Strategic and International Studies*, (Dec 2007), http://www.csis.org/component/option,com_csis_pubs/task,view/id,4236/type,1/ (accessed on December 18, 2007): XI.

the many challenges in Iraq, the principal challenge "is the integration of the interagency effort to ensure that progress is made along all lines of operation – not just security, but economic, governance, and the rule of law as well."[7] In his role as Combined Arms Center Commander, then Lieutenant General Petraeus supported the development of the Army doctrinal manual FM 3-24, *Counterinsurgency*, which cites the importance of a unified interagency effort. FM 3-24 has an entire chapter entitled "Unity of Effort: Integrating Civilian and Military Activities," which details the principles of effective civilian and military cooperation in a counterinsurgency fight.[8]

Then LTG Petraeus's achievements in promoting awareness about interagency cooperation in counterinsurgency, identified by the acronym COIN, assisted in the development of a similar interagency counterinsurgency guide. The Departments of State and Defense along with the US Agency for International Development (USAID) published the Final Draft Interim COIN guide in late 2007.[9] The main focus of this publication is COIN, but it provides very useful operational level principles that are applicable to all expeditionary interagency operations. It provides an overview of the various capabilities that each government agency has available which could support interagency expeditionary operations. The DOD capabilities that are described in the COIN guide are based in large part on the results of a DOD process called the Quadrennial Defense Review (QDR).

---

[7] Senate Committee on Armed Services, *Nomination hearing for LTG David H. Petraeus to be General, and Commander Multi-National Force Iraq,* 110th Cong., 1st sess., 2007, 3, http://armed-services.senate.gov/statemnt/2007/January/Petraeus%2001-23-07.pdf (accessed November 3, 2007).

[8] Department of the Army, *FM 3-24 Counterinsurgency,* (Washington DC: Department of the Army, December 2006) Chap. 2.

[9] Stephen Mull, Michael Vickers, and Michael Hess, *Counterinsurgency for US Government Policy Makers: A Work in Progress,* Department of State Publication 11456: Bureau of Political-Military Affairs (Washington DC: 2007), http://www.usgcoin.org/library/USGDocuments/InterimCounterinsurgencyGuide(Oct2007).pdf (accessed November 15, 2007).

The 2006 Quadrennial Defense Review outlines four main priorities used to shape US military capabilities in the years ahead: defeating terrorist networks, defending the homeland in depth, shaping the choices of countries at strategic crossroads, and preventing hostile states and non-state actors from acquiring or using Weapons of Mass Destruction (WMD). These priorities nest well with the NSCT. US military capabilities can achieve some limited operational goals in combating terrorism, but the NSCT requires unified US government interagency action and the partnership of many nations.

Citing the need for partner nations to assist in combating terrorism, the NSCT asserts that "success will not come by always acting alone, but through a powerful coalition of nations maintaining a strong unified international front against terrorism."[10] Among these partner nations there are those that have the will but not the capability to support the GWOT. Addressing this lack of capabilities is a stated objective of the NSCT, and a decisive strategic foreign policy objective of the Department of State.[11] However, because of limited resources the US attempted to prioritize the pivotal areas in which to provide assistance.

These pivotal areas are described by noted Transnational Crime expert Phil Williams, as capacity gaps or functional holes.[12] Functional holes are areas of weak governance in a state that is connected to the global economic system. Once established in these gaps or holes, criminal or terrorist organizations may use their position to exploit the global economic system for profit and funds to further their illicit activities. The types and numbers of these functional holes vary from

---

[10] George Bush, "National Strategy for Combating Terrorism," 2003, 19.

[11] US Department of State, "FY 2006 Performance and Accountability Highlights," under "2006 Performance Indicator I," http://www.state.gov/s/d/rm/rls/perfrpt/2006hlts/html/79818.htm (accessed November 4, 2007).

[12] Phil Williams, "Combating Transnational Organized Crime," in *Transnational Threats: Blending Law Enforcement and Military Strategies*, ed. Carolyn Pumphrey, (Carlisle, PA: Strategic Studies Institute, 2000), 192.

nation to nation. Two of the most important functional holes which are relevant to the GWOT are counter terrorism and border security.

Much of the US government's assistance to partner nations, to date, focuses on counter terrorism training. In fiscal year 2006, the Department of State facilitated the conduct of "counterterrorism training for 77 partner nations and performed 269 training events."[13] This training focused on the capability of partner nations to conduct counter terrorism activities within their nations. While this is an important capability, a more important focus of US government assistance should be to enhance US partners' abilities to secure their territorial borders.

One important way in which states assert control over territory is through border security, yet many partner nations "do not have the law enforcement, intelligence, or military capabilities to assert effective control over their entire territory."[14] A lack of effective border security is especially troubling in the context of the GWOT. The NSCT cites this threat as one of its priorities of action, "deny terrorist entry to the US and disrupt their travel internationally."[15] The National Strategy to Combat Terrorist Travel expands this objective to include providing financial and technical assistance to "assist partner nations in using their intelligence and law enforcement capabilities to detect terrorist movements across and within their borders, and to disrupt terrorist travel facilitation networks."[16]

In order to expand its scope and capability, a transnational terrorist organization must move supplies and personnel between nations. Uninhibited movement across international borders of enslaved persons, WMD materials, terrorist personnel and equipment, drugs,

---

[13] Ibid, 1.

[14] George Bush, National Strategy for Combating Terrorism, (Washington DC: White House, February, 2003), 20.

[15] Ibid, 13.

[16] National Counter Terrorism Center, "National Strategy to Combat Terrorist Travel," May 2, 2006, under "Strategic Objective 2: Help Partner Nations Build Capacity to Limit Terrorist Travel," http://www.nctc.gov/docs/u_terrorist_travel_book_may2_2006.pdf13 (accessed on December 16, 2007).

conventional weapons, and black market commodities gives these terrorist organizations the opportunity to expand their activities and also creates and sustains instability in the areas they operate. Another concerning post-9/11 report indicated that terrorists, drug traffickers, human traffickers and transnational criminal gangs are already using the same transnational movement and supply routes.[17] Terrorists and criminal organizations are forming alliances based on perceived common goals in states that lack effective border security. This convergence of illicit organizations represents a threat to US National Security and requires a renewed focus on border security.

Border security operations and training activities typically fall within the realm of law enforcement agencies. The US Foreign Assistance Act prohibits training of law enforcement forces in foreign nations by the DOD, but the President, by declaration, may override these prohibitions. There is also a bill before Congress titled "The Building Global Partnership Act," which would grant the DOD the flexibility to train foreign forces such as "coast guards, gendarmes, paramilitary, border police, civil defence and other forces that typically fall under the control of the local Ministry of the Interior (MOI)."[18] Until Congress takes action on the proposed bill, the requirements for maintaining current law enforcement operations as well training additional border troops, far exceeds the capabilities of other US government agencies and most partner nations. A US government interagency team, led by the US military, which is capable of training other nation's border troops, equipping these troops, and providing military assistance to build border security infrastructure would help close this gap in capabilities. This initiative could result in a measurable decrease in the scope and capability of global terrorist networks to conduct destabilizing activities which threaten the national security interests of the US and its allies.

---

[17] Tamara Makarenko, "Transnational crime and its evolving links to terrorism and instability," *Jane's Intelligence Review*, (November 2001) 22.

[18] Hicks and Morrison, 10.

An initiative of this type will also provide other benefits for the US and its partner nations: in the area of legitimacy and credibility, and economic development. Concerning the former, a 2003 NY Times article summarizing interviews and surveys from around the world stated "the widespread and fashionable view is that the United States is a classically imperialist power bent on controlling global oil supplies and on military domination."[19] Furthermore, among developing nations, US military assistance is often viewed as lacking a long-term development approach. It is perceived as a means to gain a temporary alliance to accomplish a foreign policy objective or even as a way to exploit the resources of the developing nation. In the Middle East the perception of the US is particularly challenging, as shown by a 2005 Pew Research poll that cited Anti-Americanism in the region as being driven largely by "the general perception that the U.S. fails to consider the interests of countries in the region when it acts in the international arena."[20]

The US could begin to address its legitimacy and credibility within the United Nations as it supports the United Nations General Assembly's Counter-Terrorism Strategy and commitment to end human trafficking. The UN Counter-Terrorism strategy states that nations will

> Step-up national efforts and bilateral, sub-regional, regional and international co-operation, as appropriate, to improve border and customs controls, in order to prevent and detect the movement of terrorists and to prevent and detect the illicit traffic in, inter alia, small arms and light weapons, conventional ammunition and explosives, nuclear, chemical, biological or radiological weapons and materials, while recognizing that States may require assistance to that effect.[21]

---

[19] Richard Bernstein, "Two Years Later: World Opinion; Foreign Views of U.S. Darken After Sept.11," *New York Times*, Sep 11, 2003, http://query nytimes.com/gst/fullpage html?res=9B02E2DE133BF932A2575AC0A9659C8B63&sec=&spon=&pagewanted=2 (accessed on Dec 18, 2007).

[20] Andrew Kohut, "Arab and Muslim Perceptions of the U.S.," Pew Research Center (Nov 10, 2005), http://pewresearch.org/pubs/6/arab-and-muslim-perceptions-of-the-united-states (accessed on Dec 18, 2007).

[21] UN General Assembly, "Global Counter-Terrorism Strategy," (New York: 2006), http://www.un.org/terrorism/index.shtml (accessed November 11, 2007).

Likewise, in support of the UN effort to end human trafficking, Secretary of State Condoleezza Rice reaffirmed the US resolve by stating that, "All nations that are resolute in the fight to end human trafficking have a partner in the United States."[22] By visibly assisting other nations to secure their borders it will support US and UN policy with credible actions and regain international credibility that was negatively impacted by the invasion of Iraq. In addition to its impact on the United Nations, the US initiative would advance the credibility of the US within the specific partner nations. Helping to improve the capabilities of partner nations to secure their sovereign territorial borders may reverse the negative perceptions of the US and facilitate the development of strong enduring partnerships.

The second area of benefit for the US and its partners engaged in improving border security is economic development. Securing borders could promote the economic development of the partner-nations and create stronger economic partners for the US. This economic development would result from a reversal of four negative economic impacts that are a result of ineffective border security; poor revenue collection, poor worker productivity, corruption of financial and public institutions and diversion of resources.[23]

Poor customs and tariffs collection from the legal or illegal transit of commercial goods across national borders is a significant loss of potential revenue for a partner-nation. A 1999 World Bank report estimated that the worldwide revenue loss from illegal tobacco smuggling alone was over $28 billion.[24] If one examines individual countries with porous borders such as Pakistan, the impacts are even more pronounced. In Pakistan it is estimated that 40% of the local

---

[22] US Department of State, *Trafficking in Persons Report*, (June 2007), under "Secretary of State Rice's Introduction," http://www.state.gov/documents/organization/82902.pdf (accessed on December 17, 2007).

[23] Phil Williams and Ernesto U. Savona, eds., *The United Nations and Transnational Crime* (London: Frank Cass &Co, 1996), 32-38.

[24] The World Bank Group, Curbing the Epidemic: Governments and the Economics of Tobacco Control, (Washington, 1999), http://www1.worldbank.org/tobacco/reports_pdf.asp 63-64 (accessed December 2, 2007).

tea consumption is smuggled tea which represents a $2.5 million annual loss in customs revenue for the Pakistani government.[25]

In areas where border security is weak it is also likely that there will be poorer worker productivity. The populations in these areas are often sold or given drugs in return for services they may provide to assist the traffickers, and as a result there are substantial user populations in these areas.[26] Drug use not only results in a loss in short term worker productivity but will likely add to the long term health care costs of these workers. Additionally, worker productivity is affected by the violent nature of many of the transactions associated with illegal border traffic. Simply put, the higher the value of the goods being smuggled the more likely the smugglers will go to any length to protect their cargo, finances, or their freedom of movement in a region. For example, in Mexico it was reported that there were 2,308 narcotics related executions in the first nine months of 2007.[27]

Corruption of financial and public institutions also represents a negative economic impact for partner-nations. Transnational criminal and terrorist organizations, handle a large amount of cash from their illegal transactions. In many cases the storage and global movement of this cash requires the use of legitimate financial institutions. However, in order to avoid detection the illicit organizations must corrupt officials in these legitimate financial institutions. This corruption has multiple effects: it undermines public confidence; erodes the capacity of a

---

[25] Romail Kenneth, "Tea smuggling from Afghanistan deprives govt of Rs 152m revenue," *Daily Times* May 11, 2007, http://www.dailytimes.com.pk/default.asp?page=2007%5C05%5C11%5Cstory_11-5-2007_pg5_8 (accessed Nov 15, 2007).

[26] Williams and Savona, 33.

[27] Foreign Military Studies Office / Joint Reserve Intelligence Center Border Security Team, "More than Two Thousand Narco-Executions in 2007," *Mexico, Central America, and Caribbean Newsbriefs*, Sep 25, 2007.

government to manage, control and regulate financial systems; and creates unnecessary restrictions of legitimate financial activities.[28]

The fourth area of economic impact is the diversion of resources. Developing nations in general have a relatively small capacity to generate revenue for their governments which then could be used to provide services to their people. As demonstrated in preceding paragraphs, the smuggling of goods limits this revenue even further. So with limited revenues and increased violence, larger proportions of the budget are used to provide basic internal and external security for the people and the government. US assistance targeted toward improving border security could help reduce this diversion of resources.

Methodology

By first demonstrating the convergence of global terrorist networks with other illicit networks the paper establishes the threat posed to the interests of the US and its allies. It uses analysis of trends in two regions; Tri-border area (TBA) of Paraguay, Brazil, and Argentina, and the Trans Sahel (TS) region in Africa to determine the threat from what Tamara Makarenko calls the Crime-Terror-Continuum (CTC). The important aspect of the CTC studied here, is the ability to exploit ineffective border security in an area and destabilize a nation state or region.[29]

The paper then examines the specific challenges presented in conducting border security operations and training in areas affected by the CTC. Three case studies were chosen to assist in establishing the principles and tenets of effective border security operations and training. The first case study discusses the US occupation of Germany after WWII and demonstrates the diplomatic, informational, economic and military challenges of border security operations

---

[28] Williams and Savona, 37.

[29] Tamara Makarenko, "The Crime-Terror Continuum: Tracing the Interplay between Transnational Organized Crime and Terrorism," *Global Crime,* Vol. 6, No. 1, (February 2004), http://www.silkroadstudies.org/new/docs/publications/Makarenko_GlobalCrime.pdf (accessed on November 17, 2007), 138.

following major combat. The second case study examines the Israeli Border Guards and demonstrates best practices for training and development of a border security force. The final case study uses the border security operations and training principles from Germany and Israel to examine the effectiveness of African border security initiatives in the context of the GWOT. From the analysis of all three case studies this paper makes recommendations which provide the foundation for Joint or Interagency doctrine and/or the framework for a change in focus for GCC Theater Security Cooperation activities.

Definitions

To assist in the development of this paper the explanation of the following key terms assist in framing the discussion: *expeditionary, Theater Security Cooperation Activities,* and *Border Security Operations.* The definition used for the term *expeditionary* is from Joint Publication 1-02, which states that an expeditionary force "is an armed force organized to accomplish a specific objective in a foreign country."[30] The interagency portion of a Border Security Team would complement the military capabilities of the team and would need to be fully deployable.

In referring to *Theater Security Cooperation Activities,* the paper uses the Joint Publication 3-0 definition below:

> Military activity that involves other nations and is intended to shape the operational environment in peacetime. Activities include programs and exercises that the US military conducts with other nations to improve mutual understanding and improve interoperability with treaty partners or potential coalition partners. They are designed to support a combatant commander's theater strategy as articulated in the theater security cooperation plan[31]

---

[30] Office of Joint Chiefs of Staff, *JP 1-02, Dictionary of Military and Associated Terms,* (Washington DC: Chairman Joint Chiefs of Staff 2001), 151.

[31] Office of Joint Chiefs of Staff, *JP 3-0 Joint Operations* (Washington DC: Chairman Joint Chiefs of Staff 2006), GL-28.

The term *Border Security Operations* is not defined in any current US military doctrine, but a partial definition is found in the obsolete US Army Field Manual 31-55 from 1972 titled *Border Security and Anti-Infiltration Operations.* FM 31-55 defines Border Security as, "steps taken to counter any threat posed by an exterior force illegally attempting to cross international borders."[32] In order to complete this definition the paper incorporates the Joint Publication 1-02, *Dictionary of Military and Associated Terms*, definition of security: "A condition that results from the establishment and maintenance of protective measures that ensure a state of inviolability from hostile acts or influences."[33] Combined together these definitions allow for a more comprehensive view of border security to include not just illegal crossings, but also those activities designed to negatively influence activity on the border between two nations.

Limitations

This study recognizes that border security operates in many different environments and the threats to national borders utilize all available means to penetrate the territorial sovereignty of a nation. However, given the focus of the research question, the paper does not examine border security issues associated with territorial borders along coastal regions. Although one could argue that the same principles and tenants apply to these coastal regions since the negative impacts of poor border security and the threats remain the same. Secondly, the paper seeks to deal only with those nations with large capability gaps in border security and with whom the US enjoys a functioning partnership, while recognizing the need to address the activities of recalcitrant States in proximity to our partner states. Finally, the paper does not address the many additional border security initiatives between the US and countries such as Canada and the European Union which are within the capability of law enforcement agencies to address.

---

[32] U.S. Department of the Army, *FM 31-55, Border Security and Anti-Infiltration Operations,* (Washington DC: Department of the Army, March 1972), 1-1.

[33] Office of Joint Chiefs of Staff, JP 1-02, 381.

Threat Convergence

The Rise of the Transnational Criminal Organization

The nation state itself is the new battleground for the 21st century. The shifting paradigms of national security since the end of the Cold War and, more notably, post 9/11 have moved from a geopolitical analysis of interstate conflict to an intrastate conflicts and conflicts with non-state actors. Gone are the days of Cold War *Realpolitik* in a bipolar world. Of the 139 conflicts since the end of the Cold War only 10 have been classified as interstate conflicts.[34] While the actors in these conflicts typically reside in the particular state, they increasingly rely on external resources like people, money and weapons to sustain their fight. In return for these instruments of conflict the state itself is gutted of its valuable natural and financial resources to pay for the external support.

It is important to distinguish the difference between the actors who execute the conflict and those that provide the conduits for resource movement. The actors who have the expertise to move illegal resources into and out of conflict areas and throughout the globe are members of Transnational Criminal Organizations (TCO). Participants in these organizations are "associated for the purpose of engaging in sustained criminal activity which requires the movement of information, money, physical objects, people or other tangible or intangible items across state boundaries."[35] These TCOs must use various legitimate institutions to support their activities. Frequently, these legitimate institutions are in the financial sector.

Most criminal transactions require the movement of currency into and out of a legitimate global financial system. Money laundering, as it is commonly referred, is a problem of elusive scope. It is estimated that money laundering represents somewhere between two to five percent

---

[34] Monty G. Marshall, "Major Episodes of Political Violence 1946-2006," Center for Systemic Peace, (September 18, 2007), http://www.systemicpeace.org/warlist htm (accessed October 11, 2007).

[35] Williams and Savona, 4.

of world Gross Domestic Product, or using 2006 figures, between $1.3 and $3.3 trillion dollars.[36] Such a sum cannot be hidden under the proverbial mattress, it requires the use of legitimate financial institutions connected to world markets. TCOs "clean" this money and use it for investments in real estate, financial markets and consumption. What has enabled these financial transactions, as well as TCO movement of goods and people, is the fast pace of globalization since the end of the Cold War.

The fall of the Berlin Wall in November 1989 began a process of global economic expansion. In his 2006 book, *The World is Flat,* Thomas Freidman describes conceptually how the fall of the wall brought about the defeat of the main economic obstacle to free markets-Communism- and also allowed many nations, and unfortunately criminal organizations, to see the world "as more of a seamless whole."[37] A criminal enterprise, similar to a legitimate business, seeks to offer a unique product and to capture the largest share of the market for that product. The criminal organizations saw the global market as a way to do both. Organizations began to specialize in various activities that were needed to conduct criminal activity transnationally. Some groups became experts in human smuggling, others in document forgery. Still others had financial specialties. They also began expanding their influence through the newly liberated world by seeking to establish or expand markets for their criminal specialties. This expansion transformed these criminal organizations into what has been defined as TCOs.

As the TCOs expanded globally, a network of supply and shipping routes and warehousing locations began to develop. The supply and shipping routes relied on traditional smuggling routes, but also expanded along newly developed legitimate infrastructure. As these organizations expanded in scope they required more warehousing space for their products as well.

---

[36] Organization for Economic Co-operation and Development, "Ten years of combating money laundering," *OECD Observer,* (October 1999), http://www.oecdobserver.org/news/fullstory.php?aid=63 (accessed November 19, 2007).

[37] Thomas Freidman, *The World is Flat*, (New York: Farrar, Strauss and Giroux, 2006), 51.

While some of these routes and warehouses existed in developed nations, the vigilant law enforcement of these nations made operating costs high for a TCO. The TCOs needed a nation that either passively or actively allowed these organizations to conduct major logistical operations in and through their national territory. These passive nation states with weak and corruptible institutions were the perfect vehicle for TCOs to influence through outright coercion and corruption. These nation states would come to be known as failed states.

A failed state has three elements: an internal or endogenous implosion specific to its territory; the near or total breakdown of structures guaranteeing law and order; and, the absence of institutions capable of representing the state at the international level or of being influenced by the outside world.[38] Failed states are nations such as Somalia and Sierra Leone who, for years, were completely lawless and chaotic. Failed States can also be states such as Thailand and Costa Rica whose governmental institutions are corrupt and unwilling or unable to resist the power of TCOs. One of the government institutions of most interest to TCOs is the Border Police which, when in existence, typically controls the flow of people and goods in and out of the failed state. Control of this institution allows the TCO to complete the link to its global logistics network and transport people and material across international borders. As this evolution of TCOs took place other organizations began to see a convergence of their interests. One such converging type of organization was the Global Terrorist Network (GTN).

The Crime-Terror Continuum

The development of converging interests between TCOs and GTNs is not a static process. Evolving for more than a decade, Tamara Makarenko characterizes this process as the Crime-

---

[38] Daniel Thurer, "The 'failed State' and international law," *International Review of the Red Cross* No. 836, (Dec. 31, 1999), http://www.icrc.org/web/eng/siteeng0 nsf/html/57JQ6U (accessed on Nov 17, 2007).

Terror Continuum (CTC).[39] Figure 1 helps describe the placement of the groups on the continuum and the various types of activities that indicate a convergence of their interests. The far ends of the spectrum represent these two types of groups operating independently. Depending on the goals and needs of these organizations they will move along this continuum at various times with a greater degree of convergence, culminating with a complete convergence of interests and activities.

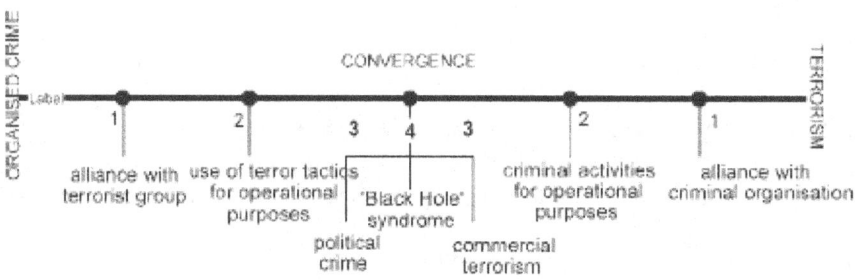

Figure 1-Crime Terror Continuum *Source* Tamara Makarenko, The Crime-Terror Continuum: Tracing the Interplay between Transnational Organized Crime and Terrorism," *Global Crime,* Vol. 6, No. 1, February 2004, 131.

. Before discussing the convergence it is important to note other categories of relationships between these two groups. The first level of relationships on the CTC is the alliance. These alliances can be long-term partnerships or merely one-time arrangements to seek specialized knowledge or gain operational support.[40] For a short-term alliance the terrorist can tap into the existing smuggling routes and money-laundering apparatus of the criminal organizations and the criminal organization can utilize the operational planning and terrorist tactics of a terrorist group. An example of this comes from Columbia where it was reported that the Medellin drug cartel hired the ELN terrorist group to plant car bombs.[41] Beyond these short-term alliances, is a more substantial type of long-term cooperation which is beneficial to both

---

[39] Makarenko, "The Crime-Terror Continuum: Tracing the Interplay between Transnational Organized Crime and Terrorism," 130.

[40] Ibid, 131.

[41] Ibid, 131.

types of organizations. In 2001, it was reported that "militants linked to Al Qaeda also

established connections with Bosnian organized crime figures…Al Qaeda and the Taliban found

a route for the trafficking of heroin from Afghanistan into Europe through the Balkans."[42] Al

Qaeda used the criminal organization's existing smuggling routes for a fee and in return found

new markets in Europe for Afghan heroin to produce operational funds for their terrorist

activities.

Once these longer-term alliances are formed it is in the interests of both groups to

maintain an environment which is conducive to their cooperative activities. This environment of

instability exists in what previously was defined as a failed state and is critical to success for

these groups. Instability in a failed state is in the interest of terrorists for the continued existence

of sanctuary activities and it is of interest of criminal groups seeking to maintain their logistics

supply chain for its criminal operations. So in addition to activities conducted transnationally,

these groups must cooperate on destabilizing activities in the failed states.

The second level of relationship occurs when the TCOs and GTNs use each others

operational tools to achieve their goals. When possible each type of illicit group would prefer to

use its internal resources to achieve its goals. They may ally with one another only temporarily

until they can develop the desired capability within their organization. Again, there is a striking

resemblance to legitimate business activities. These groups are determining the capabilities

required to support their growing businesses and determining whether it makes sense to outsource

these capabilities or to develop them internally. For example, Mexican drug cartels regularly

conduct kidnapping and assassinations of other cartel members as well as police and government

---

[42] Kurt Eichenwald, "A Nation Challenged: The Money; Terror Money Hard to Block, Officials Find," *New York Times* December 10, 2001, http://query nytimes.com/gst/fullpage html?res=9D0DEFDF163FF933A25751C1A9679C8B63&sec=&spon=&pagewanted=all (accessed November 18, 2007).

officials.[43] These groups have learned this terrorist operational tool and no longer have to outsource. Also, at the other end of the Crime-Terror Continuum, there is evidence that Al Qaeda's financial network in Europe relies on credit card fraud to generate nearly $1 million a month.[44]

Makarenko's third level on the Crime-Terror Continuum occurs when criminal and terrorist groups converge into a single entity that displays characteristics of both types of groups and can potentially transform itself into the type of group at the opposite end of the continuum from which it began.[45] In this convergence area there are criminal groups that display political motivations and terrorist groups that become interested in the profits from criminal activities and maintain their political rhetoric as a front to continue their criminal activities. The example used for this first type of group would be the Albanian Mafia in the late 1990s. The Albanian Mafia and Kosovo Liberation Army collaborated together to such a degree that their members were interchangeable.[46] The Mafia needed a broader base of support to destabilize the government and the KLA needed the money the Mafia could provide. Over a period of time they converged in the center of the Crime-Terror Continuum. In a similar manner, Abu Sayef ran successful marijuana plantations in the Philippines and in many respects no longer seeks to achieve its original political aims, but only to perpetuate its terrorist façade in order to maintain a recruitment base.[47]

The final area of Makarenko's Crime-Terror Continuum thesis is the black hole syndrome, which refers to situations where "failed states foster the convergence between transnational organized crime and terrorism, and ultimately create a safe haven for the continued

---

[43] Foreign Military Studies Office / Joint Reserve Intelligence Center Border Security Team, "Daily News Summary," *Mexico, Central America, and Caribbean Newsbriefs*, Sep 28, 2007.

[44] Rohan Gunaratna, *Inside Al Qaeda: Global Networks of Terror* (New York: Hurst & Company 2006), 65.

[45] Makarenko, "The Crime-Terror Continuum: Tracing the Interplay between Transnational Organized Crime and Terrorism," 135.

[46] Ibid, 136.

[47] Ibid, 137.

operations of the convergent groups."[48] Under this definition, Afghanistan, prior to the US-invasion, and Sierra Leone, prior to UN intervention, were good examples of the black hole syndrome. While very few states descend all the way to a "black hole," many weak states exhibit so many characteristics that not much effort would be required to push them completely into the "black hole." Likewise, many weak states have specific areas within their borders that exhibit characteristics that would justify calling them intrastate "black holes."

Whether the failed states are symptomatic of the "black hole" syndrome or merely have intrastate "black holes" addressing the threats of the CTC in these areas should be a priority of the US national security strategy as well as the International community's security strategy. A "black hole" failed state would likely require a larger expenditure of resources over an extended period of time to stabilize and reintegrate into the international community. It is therefore desirable for the US to address threats in vital partner nations early to prevent the costly and tragic descent of a nation into a failed state or into "black hole" state.

Addressing this threat would also require a US national security strategy that integrates the various subordinate strategies of US departments and agencies into a comprehensive approach to addressing the CTC threat. The 2007 CSIS report on Non traditional Security Assistance argues that there is no such comprehensive approach, "the task force identifies a lack of coherent strategic vision and authoritative planning on CT matters across DOD, State and other relevant U.S. government departments."[49] During the development of this paper a similar review was conducted and of the various US strategy documents there were eight different published strategy documents which relate to this CTC threat; The National Strategy to Combat Terrorism, National Drug Control Strategy, National Border Patrol Strategy, National Military Strategy to Combat Terrorism, Anti terrorism Assistance Program, National Strategy for Combating Weapons of

---

[48] Ibid 138.

[49] J. Stephen Morrison and Kathleen Hicks, 7.

Mass Destruction, The Export Control and Related Border Security Program Strategic Plan, and the National Strategy to Combat Terrorist Travel. Each of these strategies addressing the unique aspects of the CTC which are within the capability of each agency to address, however, the lack of a unifying strategic document for all of these agencies appears to result in a less than optimal approach to the CTC problem.

The CTC in the Trans Sahel

The Sahel region of Africa borders the Sahara Desert to the north and the tropical regions to its south. It spans almost the entire width of Africa and it reaches across 10 nation states. The region is also one of the poorest in Africa due to its harsh landscape and climate, and a lack of natural resources. Many of the inhabitants of this region are nomadic tribes who do not conform easily to the boundaries of the nation state system. The governments of the nations of the Sahel are poorly-resourced to provide any, let alone effective, enforcement of their territorial borders. These conditions meet the first criteria of the CTC; what previously has been identified as areas of weak governance or seams which are open to exploitation by criminal and terrorist groups. Due to its location and lack of connectivity with the larger global community, the Sahel may not seem a good candidate for establishing large scale illicit logistical bases, but does provide viable transnational supply routes for illicit goods. Figure 2 shows how this region has traditionally been used for the facilitation of trade across the continent.

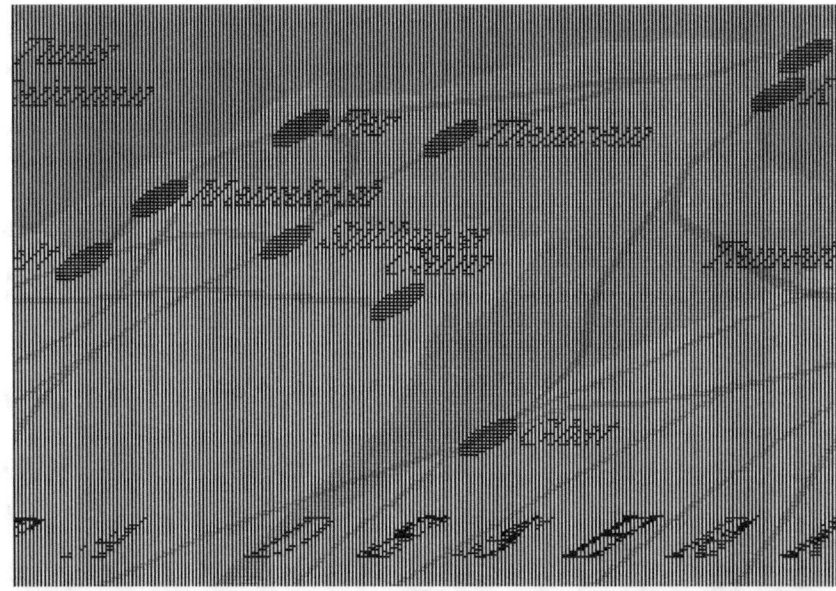

Figure 2 Traditional Trans Sahara Trade Routes *Source*: Mike Dowling, "Mr. Dowling's Ancient African Trade Page," (April 2, 2006) http://www mrdowling.com/609-trade html (accessed November 14, 2007).

One particular terrorist group the *Groupe Salafiste pour la Predication et le Combat,* known formerly as GSPC, or Al Qaeda in the land of the Islamic Maghreb (AQIM) has capitalized on the Trans Sahel seam. Using traditional trade routes, the AQIM has financed its terrorist operations against the Algerian government primarily through the smuggling of cigarettes and people.[50] The AQIM transports cigarettes from West Africa through the Sahel and then Algeria on route to Europe where the cigarettes are sold. In addition to cigarettes, the AQIM acts as paid security escorts for groups wishing to smuggle people, arms or drugs along these same routes, which represents the second criteria of the CTC an operational alliance between terrorists and criminal groups. The profits from these joint activities are then used to fund further AQIM and criminal activities. Properly exhibiting the criteria of Makarenko's CTC model, the GTC has converged into a dangerous single entity which moves back and forth along the continuum conducting terrorist and criminal activities which destabilize the region.

The CTC in East Africa

Across the continent of Africa another area faces similar challenges related to the CTC. East Africa offers TCOs and GTNs a geographic proximity to the Middle East and Asia with a large coastline and desolate interior areas. Like the Sahel, East Africa is not a conducive area for connecting to the global economic infrastructure, but rather for use as a transit and supply area.

---

[50] Mary Jo Choate, "Trans-Sahara Counterterrorism Initiative: Balance of Power?" (USAWC Strategic Research Project, U.S. Army War College, 2007), http://stinet.dtic.mil/oai/oai?&verb=getRecord&metadataPrefix=html&identifier=ADA469176 (accessed October 20, 2007).

"The East African coast is open, poorly patrolled, and easily accessible to small watercraft that can make landfall almost at will. Together with the population, urban settlements, and infrastructure of the mainland, the coast offers great advantages for legitimate traders as well as smugglers seeking access to world markets with a minimum of risk."[51]

The countries of Somalia and Sudan in particular are States that meet the first criterion of the CTC model as they actively and passively support TCO and GTN activity. Al Qaeda has operated training camps in the Sudan in the past and conducted operations against targets in neighboring Kenya and Tanzania. Through established smuggling routes in Kenya and Somalia, TCOs move illegal weapons and drugs into and through the area, fueling the insurgent movements within those countries. Although no direct alliances have been overtly discovered between the TCOs and GTNs operating in East Africa, it is clear they both are using the porous land and sea borders to their operational advantage.

The CTC in the Tri Border Area (TBA)

The region identified in Figure 3 as the Tri Border Area of South America, encompasses portions of the countries of Brazil, Argentina and Paraguay, specifically the cities of Puerto Iguazu, Argentina, Foz de Iguazu Brazil, and Ciudad del Este, Paraguay. The TBA contains a large population of foreigners, between 12,000 and 40,000 Arabs and 30,000 Asians, and has a vibrant legitimate and illegitimate economy estimated to be $12 billion per year.[52] The

---

[51] Glenn E. Curtis, "Nations Hospitable to Organized Crime and Terrorism," Library of Congress (Washington, D.C: U.S. Government Printing Office, 2003), http://www.loc.gov/rr/frd/pdf-files/Nats_Hospitable.pdf (accessed February 7, 2007) 10.

[52] Rex Hudson, *Terrorist and Organized Crime Groups in the Tri-Border Area (TBA) of South America*, Library of Congress (Washington, D.C.: US Government Printing Office, 2003), under "The General Population of the TBA," http://www.loc.gov/rr/frd/pdf-files/TerrOrgCrime_TBA.pdf (accessed October 16, 2007) 7.

illegitimate economy flourishes in this region due to a lack of effective security institutions.

Figure 3-TBA Map *Source* Mike Boettcher, "South America's Tri Border Back on Terrorism Radar," Cable News Network, November 8, 2002, http://archives.cnn.com/2002/WORLD/americas/11/07/terror.triborder/ (accessed December 2, 2007). Most of the border controls between these three nations are weak and corrupt and organized

criminal groups' control of the local city governments contribute this negative security

environment in the TBA.[53] The TBA area meets the first criteria of the CTC "black hole," a

weak government that passively and actively allows Transnational Criminal Organizations and

Global Terrorist Networks to operate with impunity in a portion of these nation states. In

addition to destabilizing our partner nations of Paraguay, Brazil and Argentina and the larger

South American region, the TBA provides a base of operations and logistics from which TCOs

and GTNs can coordinate activities in closer proximity to the US.

The second characteristic of the black hole syndrome exhibited by the TBA is the

convergence of TCOs and GTNs into a single entity which then dominates a state or region. The

operations of TCOs from Brazil, Columbia, Hong Kong, Italy, Japan, Lebanon, Nigeria and

Russia alongside GTNs such as Al Qaeda and Hezbollah indicate at least the first level of CTC

relationship building of alliances.[54] It is possible that the large group of TCOs and GTNs

operating together constitute a single "entity" in the TBA which effectively controls the region.

---

[53] Ibid, 4.

[54] Ibid, 3.

The TBA and Trans Sahel region provide validation for Makarenko's Crime-Terror Continuum threat model and demonstrate the danger to US national security interests. The rise of TCOs and GTNs as a result of the rapid globalization of the world following the end of the Cold War, are each a significant threat. However, as these organizations learn from each other and cooperate to destabilize and exploit certain regions and states in the world the threat will continue to grow. In addressing this threat it is known that these organizations conduct their activities across national boundaries. It is during this vulnerable transit of materials and resources across national boundaries where effective security and law enforcement can have the greatest impact on the disruption of the main sources of sustainment for these organizations.

Historical Border Security Operations and Training
Rationale of Case Studies

The case studies were selected because each provides insights into border security operations and training. The US occupation of Germany case study demonstrates many of the challenges of conducting border security operations either as an occupying power or later as a security partner. The principles observed in this case study could assist in the operational design of future border security operations conducted by the US. It is important to note that key differences exist between the politically and economically devastated post WWII Germany and the failing states mentioned in this paper.

First, Germany was previously a world military and economic power and had the demonstrated capacity to provide for its own internal and external security, many of the failed states of 2007 have never achieved this level of competence as a nation. Second, a history of democracy and effective governance existed prior to WWII, in the case of the failed states; effective governance was only accomplished by an occupying colonial power. Finally, Germany did not exist as a nation within the context of a highly integrated and technologically advanced global community. The pressures of globalization on today's failing states simply didn't exist in 1945.

In the case study on the Israeli Border Police there are some limitations of note. Israel is unique in that for its entire existence as a nation it has faced a military threat on its borders. Today's failing states face enormous domestic challenges and even external border disputes with their neighbors, but the duration and magnitude of these threats appear small in comparison to those facing Israel. Additionally, because of this constant external threat and the voluntary migration of the majority of its citizens, Israelis in comparison to citizens in most failing states, have an unparalleled awareness of the threat and willingness to sacrifice to counter the threat. With these factors in mind the Israeli case study nonetheless provides a good foundation in the principles of developing and training a border security force which could be adapted to US training missions in the future.

US Zone of Occupation in Post World War II Germany

The end of major combat operations following the surrender of Germany resulted in the four major allied powers occupying separate zones, in which they were responsible for security against internal as well as external threats. The Americans were given a sector that included 16 million Germans, 500,000 displaced persons and had nearly 1400 miles of international and regional borders to secure.[55] The initial array of 60 divisions of American combat forces appeared to provide ample numbers of troops to conduct these security activities. American combat forces initially guarded all the valuable buildings and activities and set up roadblocks to cover all the main avenues of approach used as authorized border crossing points. With all these troops in place thousands of displaced Germans still were able to circumvent the border stations and cross into the American sector, requiring a more coherent intrastate border strategy by the

---

[55] Kendall Gott, *Mobility, Vigilance, and Justice: The US Army Constabulary in Germany, 1946-1953* (Fort Leavenworth, Kansas: Combat Studies Institute Press 2006), 6.

US. Adding to the pressure on these border stations was the departure of 11 US divisions as a result of American domestic pressure to bring American troops home.[56]

In this context, General Eisenhower announced a plan in the fall of 1945 to establish a Constabulary force whose primary role would be to "maintain general military and civilian security, assist in accomplishing the American government's objectives, and to control the borders of the US Zone of Occupation."[57] This force could provide border security in the interim before a similar German force, the *Bundesgrenzshutz*, could be developed. Although planning for such a US Constabulary force had its origins in the 1944 SHAEF operational plan ECLIPSE, it would not be operational until June of 1946, a full year following the surrender of Germany. As a result thousands of Germans entered the American zone, placing additional strain on the nascent government and devastated economy.

Diplomatic Challenges

Diplomatically, border security in Germany posed two distinct challenges. First, no effective method was developed for controlling legal movement between allied zones. This was particularly a concern between the British and American zones where Germans were attempting to return to their homes or trying to conduct legal economic activity across these zones. Different policies developed between the British and Americans based on their different philosophies. The British had a very liberal movement policy and the Americans had a much stricter policy designed to prevent further stress on an already overwhelmed displaced person camp system in their sector.[58] A diplomatic agreement signed in April 1946 eased this tension by allowing German nationals freedom of movement between Allied zones.[59] The tension created by separate

---

[56] Ibid, 10.

[57] Ibid, 10.

[58] Ibid, 7.

[59] Ibid, 7.

national interests indicates a need for consistent national agreements between allied nations conducting border security operations. Establishing these policies upfront prevents a major source of confusion at the tactical level and an unnecessary burden on military commanders.

The second diplomatic challenge was between the American and Soviet zones. As tension increased at the national level between the US and the Soviet Union it hampered the cooperation between border forces on the ground in Germany. The Soviets initially were anxious to flood the allied zones with refugees to prevent having to care for them, "often granting passes to large bodies of refugees to cross into the US zone."[60] The US border troops would deny entry to these groups and the Soviets would not allow them back into the Soviet zone, causing a humanitarian crisis as these groups were stuck in no mans land between these two military forces. In some cases Soviet troops even assisted refugees in entering the American zone illegally through gaps in the American coverage.[61] This source of tension shows the importance of integrating border security policies at the national level to address challenges with adversarial nations who may attempt to counter US efforts to enhance border security in vital areas.

Information Challenges

The main challenge faced by US occupation forces in the Information element of national power was providing sources of information for those refugees, displaced persons and others attempting illegal border crossing. "Most of the people attempting to cross the international borders were ordinary Germans who were looking for food or lost relatives."[62] Providing these people effective means for finding food distribution locations and missing person registries would greatly diminish their desperation to cross the border. Thus another important tenet of border

---

[60] Ibid, 8.

[61] Oliver J. Frederickson, *The American Military Occupation of Germany 1945-1953,* (Germany: Historical Division Headquarters, US Army Europe, 1953), 62.

[62] Kendall Gott, 24.

security operations is not only the ability to communicate with the local populace culturally and linguistically, but also the ability to provide outlets for information requirements from the local population.

Military Challenges

The military challenges for US occupation forces fell into two categories, planning and operational design. In the area of planning, early intervention proved to be an important factor in the American occupation. In the case of the Germany case study, early intervention translated into the period immediately following major combat operations. As previously mentioned, in the year prior to the establishment of the Constabulary Force, US combat forces assumed the responsibility of maintaining border security. If the Constabulary Force had immediately been employed a degradation of border security may not have occurred. However, as US forces dwindled from 3,000,000 in May of 1945 to 340,000 in July 1946, the borders became more difficult to secure.[63] By the time the Constabulary force took over border security in July 1946, displaced persons in the zone had increased from 443,000 in May 1945 to 498,000 and would continue to rise to its peak of 552,000 in December of 1946.[64] This example is relevant to the planning of major current operations such as OIF and OEF. However, early intervention is also applicable to areas with little or no major combat operations.

Areas of the world that have failed or are potentially failing and would later require major military intervention would be ideal candidates for early intervention border security assistance. Theater Security Cooperation Activities are the GCC equivalent of early intervention. They could allow the building of an effective border security apparatus to prevent the flow of

---

[63] Brian A. Libby, "Policing Germany: the United States Constabulary, 1946-1952," (PhD dissertation, University of Michigan, 1977), 36.

[64] Oliver Frederiksen, 72.

destabilizing forces into a nation and prevent a catastrophic collapse that would require major international military intervention.

In terms of operational design, the US operations in Germany provide an important principle of border security operations, the need for static and mobile border security forces. Initially the Constabulary Force established a single line of 126 posts along the border including authorized border crossing sites and fixed border posts to block access altogether.[65] In the two months of August and September 1946 alone these forces turned back 46,000 persons trying to enter the American zone, but the DP numbers in the zone continued to rise.[66] A new plan emerged in an attempt to address this problem. The plan involved maintaining the established border crossing points but dismantling the fixed border posts in favor of random mobile checkpoints at different distances behind the border. These random checkpoints disrupted the attempts by persons to cross illegally who had previously mapped a route around the fixed border posts.

The third military principle of border security operations discerned from the US occupation is the use of indigenous forces. The German border police was abolished during de-nazification, but military commanders of the US occupation army quickly realized the need to reconstitute this force. The US military government authorized the establishment of a land border police or *Bundesgrenzshutz* and by November 1945 recruiting and training of this force was well underway.[67] In March of 1946 these new border police began operating with US occupation forces and had an immediate impact. Although they were only authorized to operate against German violators, it is estimated that they were responsible for a 50% decrease in border

---

[65] Kendall Gott, 26.

[66] Ibid, 26.

[67] William E. Stacy, *US Army Border Operations in Germany: 1945-1983*, (Germany: Military History Office, US Army Europe, 1984), 13.

violations by Germans in April and May 1946.[68] Despite this success, the military government issued a policy in May disarming the Land Border police because of shooting incidents between the German border police and Russian troops. The attempt to ease border tensions with the Russians made the German border police all but ineffective and after intense lobbying by US military commanders on the border the disarmament policy was rescinded in February 1947. Full control of the German interstate and international borders was transferred to the *Bundesgrenzshutz* in 1953.

Economic Challenges

Germany faced economic challenges associated with border security operations; poor economic development and black market activities. In the first instance the Allied powers had committed to an economic reunification of Germany at the Potsdam Conference in July of 1945. The agreement stated "During the period of occupation Germany shall be treated as a single economic unit. To this end common policies shall be established in regard to...import and export programs for Germany as a whole; currency and banking, central taxation and customs; transportation and communications."[69] These economic activities required interzonal movement of goods and people to be successful. By 1946 it was becoming apparent that the tensions with the Soviet Union over ideological as well economic issues would not allow this to materialize. So in July 1946 US Secretary of State James Byrnes made a proposal, which was accepted by the British and French, to administer the US, British and French zones as one economic unit.[70] Once this agreement was reached it eliminated most of the need for people to cross zones illegally for

---

[68] Ibid, 14.

[69] Cable News Network, "CNN Perspective Series: Cold War, Potsdam Agreement," under "Episode 1: Comrades," http://www.cnn.com/SPECIALS/cold.war/episodes/01/documents/potsdam.html (accessed on Dec 12, 2007).

[70] William Stacy, 40.

legal activities. What remained as a threat was the illegal movement of persons and goods associated with black market economic activities.

The limited supply of goods and the tight border restrictions following the surrender of Germany created a lucrative opportunity for black market activities. According to Brian Libby, "Black marketeering was undoubtedly the most pervasive illegal pastime in postwar Germany."[71] US forces choose to only address the large scale criminal activity which sought to take advantage of Germans in the US zone. If the US Constabulary forces attempted to shut down all black market activity it would have resulted in great hardship for the German people. The greatest providers of black market goods were the American troops themselves. In order to curb black market participation by US troops in the summer of 1946 official barter marts were established, where soldiers could exchange goods received from home for German goods. This controversial policy was ended a year later because the barter markets were circumventing an opportunity for Germany to collect customs revenue. Nonetheless, it is important to understand upfront that border security operations involving US troops will have an impact on the local economy.

Until agricultural and industrial capacity could be restarted, and until enough supplies could be imported from the US, the small scale black market provided the population the means to barter for goods and services. Most of this black market activity by ordinary Germans decreased over time as more jobs and goods were available in the German economy. Understanding and addressing black market economic activity is an important principle of border security operations. Stopping the flows of illicit goods often hurts ordinary citizens in the border who benefit directly or indirectly from the flow of goods. Economic activity substitution must occur prior to or simultaneous to the interdiction of the flow of black market goods.

In summary, eight principles for effective border security were observed in this case study. First, a need for consistent national agreements established upfront between allied and

---

[71] Brian Libby, 59.

33

partner nations concerning border security policies. Second, the importance of integrating border security policies at the US national level to address challenges with multiple transnational threats and adversarial nations who may attempt to counter US efforts to enhance border security in vital areas. The third principle is the ability to communicate with the local populace culturally and linguistically and provide outlets for information requirements from the local population. Fourth, early intervention is necessary to prevent a catastrophic collapse that would require major international military intervention. Fifth, a border security force should have static and mobile border security forces. Sixth, the use of indigenous forces in a border security force. Seventh, there should be an integrated economic development plan. Finally, along with the economic development plan should be a graduated suppression of black market activities.

Israeli Border Police

Israel has fought to maintain its territorial boundaries since its founding as a nation state in 1948. Many of these battles have involved major combat operations, but the daily responsibility for securing the borders of Israel has fallen on the Israeli Border Police, commonly referred to as the *Magav*. As the Israeli nation state began to manage the challenges of establishing a new country, the concern of Arab infiltration into Israel was initially the responsibility of the Israel Defense Force (IDF).

After the mass migration of 300,000-400,000 Arab Palestinians out of Israel during the 1948 war, there was a sharp increase in the number of these Arab refugees attempting to infiltrate back into Israel as conditions in their temporary camps began to worsen. Many were returning to harvest crops they had planted or retrieve possessions from their previous homes, but some were returning to attack Israelis and exact revenge. From 1948 to 1952 the IDF recorded a steady increase of infiltrations peaking in 1952 with 16,000.[72] The Israelis began to see these

infiltrations as a threat to Jewish property and lives, and as Israeli settlers began to die protecting

themselves from the returning Arabs they demanded action from the IDF.

The IDF simply did not have the means to deal with this threat, their border positions

were designed to prevent invasion not infiltration. In 1949 and 1950 they attempted to arm

settlers with light weapons and hired security guards for the settlements but little changed. They

employed two types of contracted security. The first force the Israelis developed was the

ma"azim, which was responsible for perimeter patrolling and ambushing. The second force

developed was the *muhzakim,* which were hired to act as guards at the settlements. The IDF

command controlled the total force of around 2,000 through a regional IDF headquarters.[73] This

system combined with increasing border fencing was only marginally effective and very costly at

over $2.5 million in the Southern region alone.[74] Reluctantly the IDF agreed it could not solve

the problem through the use of these contracted security forces and the *Hayl HaSfar* (Border

Corps) was started.[75] From this case study discussion, it appears that a permanent, professionally

trained and managed force is an organizing principle of border security force development and is

paramount to success.

The Border Corps established new bases and conducted effective mobile patrolling in the

seam border areas between fencing Israeli settlements and IDF border positions resulting in only

4638 infiltrations in 1954 and 4,351 infiltrations in 1955.[76] As the Border Corps began to equip,

train and deploy its soldiers it was plagued by an intergovernmental battle between the IDF and

---

[72] Benny Morris, *Israel's Border Wars 1949-1956: Arab Infiltration, Israeli Retaliation, and the Countdown to the Suez War* (Oxford: Oxford University Press, 1993), 28

[73] Benny Morris, 105.

[74] Ibid, 107.

[75] Ibid, 119.

[76] Ibid, 28.

Israeli Police for control of the Border Corps. Finally in 1953, the Israeli Prime Minister Ben

Gurion proposed to the Israeli Cabinet that the Israeli National Police should have responsibility

for this border force and the Israeli Border Police were formally established in July of 1953.[77]

The general view was that the nature of the work being conducted by the Border Corps was of a

law enforcement nature and this work must conform to the standards of the National Police not

the standards of the IDF.[78] Conforming to law enforcement standards has two important

functions; first it retains the IDF's legitimacy and freedom to operate as a military force only and

second, allows the border police to operate throughout the depth of the country to accomplish

their mission. A caveat to the principle of having the National Police command and control the

border security forces is that this command and control should be decentralized. This

decentralization allows them to achieve a high degree of tactical flexibility which gives them the

ability to respond quickly to severe situations and contain them, before they develop into major

problems.[79]

The second principle of an effective border security force is a comprehensive and

adaptive training program. The Israeli Border Police have a robust basic training program which

is 16 weeks long and includes police science and duties, internal security, anti-terrorism, civics,

community policing and firearms training, consistently incorporating new techniques and

equipment.[80] The level of training received by recruits allows them to operate with self

confidence and restraint in difficult tactical conditions. In addition to basic training, many

---

[77] Ibid, 121.

[78] People's Republic of China, "Chapter VII: Border and Costal Defense," China Internet Information Center, http://www.china.org.cn/english/features/book/194476.htm (accessed on Dec 19, 2007).

[79] Eitan Meyer, "The Israeli Border Guard," *Law &Order*, (Oct 1999), http://lumen.cgsccarl.com/login?url=http://proquest.umi.com/pqdweb?did=46244368&Fmt=3&clientld=50 94&RQT=309&VName=PQD (accessed December 19, 2007), 124.

[80] David Stone, "Israeli Women Play Major Role in Israel Homeland Defense," *Women & Guns*, (July 2002), http://www.womenandguns.com/archive/old0702issue/israel0702 html (accessed on Dec 19, 2007).

specialized courses are run at the National Police's counter-terrorist school including, Close Quarter Battle (CQB) tactics, house-storming, room-clearing and VIP protection techniques.[81] These specialized courses provide a foundation for the development of its special police units such as the *Yamam* a Counter-Terror and Hostage Rescue unit, the *Yamas* a Counter-Terror Undercover Unit, the *Yamag* a Tactical Counter-Crime and Counter-Terror Rapid Deployment Unit and *Matilan* an Intelligence Gathering and Infiltrations Interception Unit. The *Magav's* cultural knowledge of the areas they operate further enhances these training programs.

The *Magav* tactical companies represent a level of diversity in its members that allows greater sensitivity toward local customs throughout Israel. Its members are men and women that come from Jewish, Christian, Druze, Bedouin and many other immigrant backgrounds giving them cultural expertise in every part of Israel. In addition, the Magav companies remain stationed in areas for lengthy periods of time to further develop the familiarity of their surroundings and build relationships with the communities they protect. The Magav are fully integrated into the society they protect and this is the third principle of an effective border security force.

A high level of awareness and sense of duty is demonstrated in the conscripts of the Israeli Border Police. However, the maturity and professionalism of its NCOs and Officers is what makes this force effectively utilize these attributes. These career policemen and women provide the framework to capitalize on the national loyalty and sense of duty displayed by the young conscripts. It is important to note here that although highly trained and supervised by a professional NCO and officer corps the young members of the Israeli Border Police have been subject to numerous Human Rights complaints, particularly by Palestinians.[82] One can argue that

---

[81] Eitan Meyer, 122.

[82] U.S. Department of State, "Israel and the Occupied territories," Bureau of Democracy, Human Rights and Labor Country Report on Human Rights 2006, http://www.state.gov/g/drl/rls/hrrpt/2006/78854.htm (accessed on Dec 20, 2007).

this is an inevitable outcome considering the Border Police operate in the seam between the Israeli and Palestinian people, at the very least it is a reminder that there must be some level of acceptable risk underwritten for a border security force, particularly in the early stages of its development.

In summary the principles of an effective border security force mentioned in this chapter are; permanent status as government organization under the command and control of the National Police, with a decentralized flexible tactical command structure, that is culturally diverse, integrated into society and specially trained and supervised by a professional cadre of mature NCOs and Officers. Using these principles and the others from the case study on Germany this paper will now examine current US border security initiatives in the GWOT.

Border Security Initiatives in support of the GWOT
East Africa

The continent of Africa traditionally poses great challenges and for many years occupies a lower priority for US foreign policy. Following the 9/11 attacks a new view of Africa emerged as a region where potential and existing areas of lawlessness could be used as terrorist sanctuaries or to facilitate terrorist logistics networks, as was the case in Afghanistan. Increased military engagement in Africa began almost immediately in two areas, East Africa and the Trans Sahel region. Combined Joint Task Force Horn of Africa (CJTF HOA) was established in October of 2002 with an off shore headquarters, before occupying a land based headquarters at Camp Lemonier in Djibouti to address the East African region.

The CJTF HOA mission although a lower profile effort to the operations in Iraq and Afghanistan, has shown clear focus and results throughout its history. One of its major objectives is to promote regional stability as a means to prosecute the GWOT.[83] Working with allied

countries from around the world and through partner nations of the Intergovernmental Agency on

Development (IGAD), Djibouti, Eritrea, Ethiopia, Kenya, Somalia, Sudan and Uganda it

enhances regional stability "through capacity-building operations such as civil affairs and

military-to-military training; engineering and humanitarian support; medical, dental and

veterinarian civil action programs (MEDCAP, DENCAP, VETCAP); security training for border

and coastal areas; and maritime training with host nations."[84]

The border security training programs emphasize small-unit infantry tactics, weapons

marksmanship, personnel searches and checkpoint operations. A recent training program was

concluded in Djibouti and its purpose was outlined by US Navy Capt. Tim Moon from CJTF

HOA, "(This training) is helping Djiboutians build capacity, so they have the ability to protect

their own borders...stop the transnational threat and control the flow of people and material in and

out of their country."[85] These programs also have a well developed Public Information and

Public Diplomacy component that provides information to the local population on the purposes of

the program and facilitates local population information requirements through the host nation

government. This type of work being conducted by the task force demonstrates the applicable

principles of early intervention, coordinated allied and partner border security policies, integrated

information and economic development, and the use of indigenous forces to provide both static

and mobile border security operations.

The CJTF-HOA program provides a basic level of border security training on a very

small scale, but if the US government could enhance this training with expertise from the US

_____

[83] Combined Joint Task Force Horn of Africa, "CJTF HOA Factsheet," (October 2007), http://www hoa.centcom mil/factsheet.asp (accessed Dec 17, 2007).

[84] Ibid, 1.

[85] Sam Smith, "U.S trains Djiboutian troops in border security," CJTF HOA press release, (May 4, 2006), http://djibouti.usembassy.gov/u.s_trains_djiboutian_troops_in_border_security_may_04_2006 (accessed on Dec 17, 2007).

Customs and Border Patrol Agency, the Department of Treasury, the Department of Justice, the

Drug Enforcement Agency, the Bureau of Alcohol, Tobacco and Firearms, and the Department of

Agriculture it would greatly magnify the impact of this program. In the absence of this

interagency assistance, these CJTF HOA sponsored partner nation military training programs

coupled with the Department of State's efforts such as the East African Counterterrorism

Initiative (EACTI) are an effective interim approach to disrupting the ability of terrorist

organizations operate and move around in East Africa.[86] CJTF HOA has established the

mechanism and access to improve border security in this vital area to US national security.

However, unless a larger proportion of US government assistance and resources are provided,

particularly in the area of economic development to displace the illegitimate economy, this

initiative for the East African nations will not develop a border security force with the

characteristics of the previously studied Israeli Border Police. Across the continent another

initiative faces similar concerns.

The Sahel Region

The Trans Sahel Counter Terrorism Initiative (TSCTI) grew out of an US European

Command (EUCOM) initiative to address the lawless areas of the Sahel region of Africa. As

mentioned in Chapter One, the Sahel region is a demonstrated area of the Crime Terror

Continuum threat that magnifies the complexity of counter terrorism efforts. The TSCTI began

as the Pan-Sahel Initiative (PSI) and was exclusively a military effort to interdict terrorist

---

[86] Jessica Piombo, "Terrorism and US Counter-Terrorism Programs in Africa: An Overview," Center for Contemporary Conflict, *Strategic Insights* Vol. VI, Issue 1, (US Naval Postgraduate School: January 2007), http://www.ccc.nps navy mil/si/2007/Jan/piomboJan07.asp (accessed on Dec 17, 2007). "EACTI was established in June 2003 as a program of the Department of State, the $100 million East Africa Counterterrorism Initiative (EACTI) provides key states in the Horn of Africa with military training to strengthen coastal, border, customs, airport, and seaport security. In addition, the Initiative plans to train law enforcement officials in East Africa."

sanctuaries in the region. EUCOM conducted basic military skills training with the partner nations to increase their capacity to provide internal security.

In 2005, the PSI transitioned into the TSCTI and the DoS officially became the lead agency in its execution. Although operating with a smaller budget than EACTI, the TSCTI also integrates the efforts of the Departments of State, Defense, Treasury, and USAID as part of an interagency team.[87] As the PSI sought to provide initial access to the region and basic military training to its partner nations the TSCTI greatly expands the US government efforts in the region.

The military training now is specifically designed to assist these nations in using these military capabilities to provide more effective border security and the TSCTI also now encompasses development assistance and expanded public diplomacy campaigns. The TSCTI also brings together the nine nations of the Sahel and Maghreb regions, Chad, Niger, Mali, Mauritania, Senegal, Tunisia, Nigeria, Algeria and Morocco to help institutionalize cooperation between these nations on matters of border security and counterterrorism. As with the EACTI, this program meets many of the principles of effective border security operations, such as early intervention, coordinated allied and partner border security policies, integrated information and economic development, and the use of indigenous forces to provide both static and mobile border security operations.

The TSCTI has built the foundation for the development of effective border security forces in the partner nations of the region. However, these border security forces currently lack many of the principle characteristics of effective border security forces demonstrated by the Israeli Border Police in this paper. Most importantly, they receive relatively little substantive border security training and as a result are no match to the threats they face. In Niger for example, the Northern border area of the country is awash in violence with the rebel group *Mouvement des Nigeriens pour la Justice* (MNJ), drug smugglers and armed bandits working

---

[87] Ibid, TSCTI budget in 2006 was $30 million.

together to destabilize the region. This desolate region is of great interest to many nations including the US because it is home to the fourth largest deposit of Uranium in the world.[88]

This region's vital importance to US national security will require more interagency resources and funding for this initiative to continue to build the border security forces of these nations. If the Nigerien example is a trend, the transnational threats are already adapting to the new border security measures and operations. The US is vulnerable to setbacks in the development of these forces if the TSCTI and EACTI do not become priorities within the new African Combatant Command and within the US government as a whole. As General Jones, then Commander of European Command states, "these efforts support the long-term strategic objectives of the Global War on Terrorism by building understanding and consensus on the terrorist threat, laying foundations for future 'coalitions of the willing,' and extending our country's security perimeter."[89]

TBA Initiatives

Unlike the Trans Sahel and East Africa, the TBA has not received the same proportion of US assistance. This is less a result of the recognition of the threat this area imposes than merely the ability to develop a partnership for effective action. Brazil, Argentina and Paraguay have all recognized the need to address some of the security challenges in this region, but vary in the willingness to accept assistance from the US. Paraguay is the recipient of the most direct US assistance, but also has the weakest border security structure. Brazil and Argentina have taken actions to enhance border security in this region, but it does not appear to be a priority for either nation.

---

[88] Abdoulaye Massalatchi, "Nigerien Rebels Free Chinese Hostage in Uranium Firm," Reuters, (Jul 11, 2007), http://africa reuters.com/top/news/usnBAN124407 html, (accessed on Dec 20, 2007).

[89] James L. Jones, *A Commander's perspective on Building the Capacity of Foreign Countries Militaries Forces,* testimony before the U.S. House of Representatives Armed Services Committee, (Apr 7, 2006), http://www.dod.mil/dodgc/olc/docs/TestJones060407.pdf (accessed Dec 20, 2007).

The best partnership mechanism that exists today in the region is the 3+1 Group. Made up Brazil, Argentina, Paraguay and the US, the 3+1 group meets quarterly to seek consensus on strategies, plans and policies to counter criminal activity and terrorism in the TBA.[90] The three US partners all view the problem from a different perspective and the 3+1 group dialogues are attempting to create a common understanding of the problem and identify potential solutions. Argentina appears to have a common perspective with the US on the scope of the CTC problem, Brazil denies the existence of terrorists in the region, and Paraguay attempts to balance the various perspectives of these three larger partners and the internal influences of the illegitimate economy.[91] Until these nations can forge a common solution framework for addressing the TBA region which encompasses the principles identified in this case study, the TBA will still remain a CTC stronghold.

Conclusion

A unique window of opportunity exists in which public and private concern over the threat from illegal immigration and terrorism have fostered a much-needed debate about the role of border security in the larger context of National Security. While much of this public debate is focused on the immediate threat as a last line of defense along the US/Mexican border, the agency responsible for this defense, the Customs and Border Patrol Agency, sees a need for a broader focus. The CBP believes it is important to disrupt the threats to US borders as far away as possible from the US.

The threats to the US border since the end of the Cold War have manifested themselves in many forms such as terrorism, drug trafficking, human smuggling, and other transnational criminal activities. These threats can converge and expand the scope and capability of many of

---

[90] Hugh Smith, "Terrorism in the Iguaza Falls Region: $100 Bills, A DIME at a time," School of Advanced Military Studies 2005, (Fort Leavenworth, KS: United States Army Command and General Staff College) 16.

[91] Ibid, 20.

the US adversaries in the Global War on Terror. In places such as the Tri Border area of South America and the Trans Sahel region in Africa, this overwhelming convergence has greatly destabilized these regions.

For the past six years the main focus of the US effort to address the threats in these regions has been through the GWOT. As the US strategy developed to prosecute the GWOT it became clear that this strategy would require both a multidisciplinary approach and the assistance of many partner nations around the globe. Despite some smaller successes in interagency operations, this area of the US strategy is still in development. Likewise, in the area of partner nation assistance, many programs such as the TSCTI and CJTF HOA capacity building programs have shown only some initial success in establishing a framework for this type of work. As work in TSCTI and CJTF HOA developed it became apparent that one specific area of partner nation capacity called border security, is critical to successfully disrupting the destabilizing threats. In these remote and unstable regions, the Department of Defense is in the best position to lead an effort to address these threats.

The Department of Defense must have assistance in this effort from many US departments and agencies which bring expertise in all the elements of national power. US government interagency teams, led by US military, which are capable of training other nation's border troops, equipping these troops, and providing military assistance to build border security infrastructure, would close this gap in partner nation capabilities and could result in a measurable decrease in the scope and capability of transnational terrorist and criminal organizations to threaten the national security of the US.

Recommendations

This paper first recommends that the United States should integrate its various national strategies at the NSC level to develop a comprehensive strategy to address the asymmetric threats to US borders. The National Strategy to Combat Terrorism, National Drug Control Strategy,

National Border Patrol Strategy, National Military Strategy to Combat Terrorism, Anti terrorism Assistance Program, National Strategy for Combating Weapons of Mass Destruction, The Export Control and Related Border Security Program Strategic Plan, and the National Strategy to Combat Terrorist Travel need to be consolidated to minimize redundancy and focus the limited resources of the US government on in depth border security strategy. To further enhance the effectiveness of this consolidated plan it should be nested within the United Nations Strategy to Combat Terrorism. This would make the disruption of the Crime-Terror nexus an internationally-supported and resourced plan.

Second, a US joint doctrine publication should be developed to codify the principles of border security operations, force development and training highlighted in the case studies. The proponency for this publication should reside with Joint Forces Command and at a minimum cover the following topics

> Threats to National Sovereignty
> Border Security Operations during Stability Operations
> Border Security Operations during Theater Security Cooperation Activities
> Border Security Planning Considerations
> Interagency support to Border Security Operations
> Expeditionary Border Security Teams
> Border Security Technology
> Indigenous Border Security Force Development
> Laws and Funding Methods Pertaining to Border Security Operations

Third, the US Army and US Marine Corps should develop the capability to train and develop foreign border security forces, facilitate the construction of necessary border security infrastructure, and make these capabilities available to Geographic Combatant Commanders during Theater Security Cooperation Activities. This would require development of an in depth knowledge of border security operations and technologies as well as a skill set in the training of indigenous military forces. Both US Special Operations Command and the US Border Patrol could assist in development of this skill set.

The fourth recommendation is to develop in each US government department or agency listed here a capability to provide a sufficient amount of deployable civilian employees with expertise in the applicable aspect of border security operations. The Border Patrol has begun to expand this capability already and uses its special tactical unit BORTAC to instruct foreign law enforcement agencies in tactical interdiction techniques (ambushes), conflict resolution (counter-sniper), and specialty-tracking and enforcement operations in rural settings.[92] Although some of these agencies have already developed this capability more assets will be needed from the US Customs and Border Patrol Agency, the Department of Justice, the Drug Enforcement Agency, the Bureau of Alcohol, Tobacco and Firearms, Department of State, US Agency for International Development, Central Intelligence Agency, Defense Intelligence Agency, the National Geospatial Intelligence Agency, and the Department of Agriculture. Each partner nation will require and request different capabilities, but figure 4 illustrates an example of how the BST might be structured.

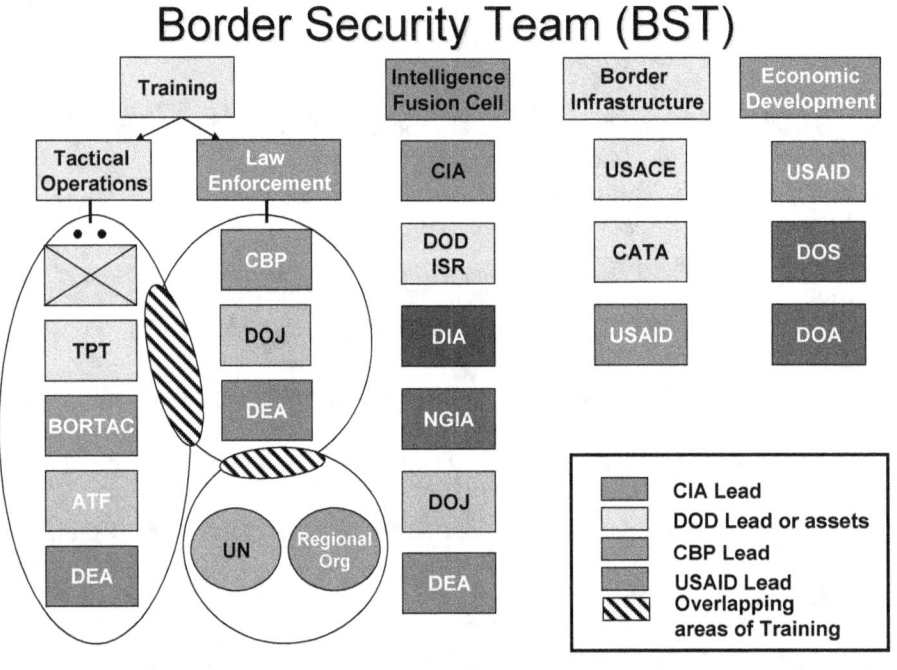

Figure 4 – Example of Border Security Team Construct

---

[92] Customs and Border Protection Agency, "BORTAC: defusing the hot spots," *Customs and Border Protection Today* (May 2004), http://www.cbp.gov/xp/CustomsToday/2004/May/bortac.xml (accessed on Dec 31, 2007).

Finally, further research will be needed in the latest border security tactics, techniques and procedures used throughout the world. As nations develop innovative solutions to counter the adaptive transnational threats, those departments and agencies involved in US border security teams must develop a process for sharing, learning and implementing new changes to stay ahead of the threats' ability to communicate its adaptations.

BIBLIOGRAPHY

Boettcher, Mike. "South America's Tri Border Back on Terrorism Radar." Cable News Network November 8, 2002. http://archives.cnn.com/2002/WORLD/americas/11/07/terror.triborder/ (accessed December 2, 2007).

Bush, George W. "National Strategy for Combating Terrorism." http://www.whitehouse.gov/news/releases/2003/02/counter_terrorism/counter_terrorism_strategy.pdf (accessed on October 17, 2007).

Choate, Mary Jo. "Trans-Sahara Counterterrorism Initiative: Balance of Power?" USAWC Strategic Research Project, U.S. Army War College, 2007. http://stinet.dtic.mil/oai/oai?&verb=getRecord&metadataPrefix=html&identifier=ADA469176 (accessed October 20, 2007).

Combined Joint Task Force Horn of Africa. "CJTF HOA Factsheet," October 2007. http://www.hoa.centcom.mil/factsheet.asp (accessed Dec 17, 2007).

Curtis, Glenn E. "Nations Hospitable to Organized Crime and Terrorism." Library of Congress Washington, D.C: U.S. Government Printing Office, 2003. http://www.loc.gov/rr/frd/pdf-files/Nats_Hospitable.pdf (accessed February 7, 2007).

Frederickson, Oliver J. *The American Military Occupation of Germany 1945-1953.* Germany: Historical Division Headquarters, US Army Europe 1953.

Freidman, Thomas. *The World is Flat.* New York: Farrar, Strauss and Giroux 2006.

Gott, Kendall. *Mobility, Vigilance, and Justice: The US Army Constabulary in Germany, 1946-1953.* Fort Leavenworth, Kansas: Combat Studies Institute Press 2006.

Gunaratna, Rohan. *Inside Al Qaeda: Global Networks of Terror.* New York: Hurst & Company 2006.

Hudson, Rex. *Terrorist and Organized Crime Groups in the Tri-Border Area (TBA) of South America.* Library of Congress Washington, D.C.: US Government Printing Office, 2003. http://www.loc.gov/rr/frd/pdf-files/TerrOrgCrime_TBA.pdf (accessed October 16, 2007).

Jones, James L. *A Commander's perspective on Building the Capacity of Foreign Countries Militaries Forces.* testimony before the U.S. House of Representatives Armed Services Committee April 7, 2006. http://www.dod.mil/dodgc/olc/docs/TestJones060407.pdf (accessed Dec 20, 2007).

Kohut, Andrew. "Arab and Muslim Perceptions of the U.S." Pew Research Center, Nov 10, 2005. http://pewresearch.org/pubs/6/arab-and-muslim-perceptions-of-the-united-states (accessed on Dec 18, 2007).

Libby, Brian A. "Policing Germany: the United States Constabulary, 1946-1952." PhD dissertation, University of Michigan, 1977.

Makarenko, Tamara. "The Crime-Terror Continuum: Tracing the Interplay between Transnational Organized Crime and Terrorism." *Global Crime* Vol. 6, No. 1 (February 2004). http://www.silkroadstudies.org/new/docs/publications/Makarenko_GlobalCrime.pdf (accessed on November 17, 2007), 122-145.

Makarenko, Tamara. "Transnational crime and its evolving links to terrorism and instability," Jane's Intelligence Review. Vol. 13 No. 11 Nov. 1 2001. 22-24.

Marshall, Monty G. "Major Episodes of Political Violence 1946-2006." Center for Systemic Peace September 18, 2007. http://www.systemicpeace.org/warlist.htm (accessed October 11, 2007).

Meyer, Eitan. "The Israeli Border Guard." *Law &Order* Oct 1999. http://lumen.cgsccarl.com/login?url=http://proquest.umi.com/pqdweb?did=46244368&Fmt=3&clientld=5094&RQT=309&VName=PQD (accessed December 19, 2007).

Morris, Benny. *Israel's Border Wars 1949-1956: Arab Infiltration, Israeli Retaliation, and the Countdown to the Suez War.* Oxford: Oxford University Press, 1993.

Morrison, J. Stephen and Kathleen Hicks, "Integrating 21st Century Development and Security Assistance," *Final Report of the Task Force on Non-Traditional Security Assistance, Center for Strategic and International Studies,* (Dec 2007), http://www.csis.org/component/option,com_csis_pubs/task,view/id,4236/type,1/ (accessed on December 18, 2007).

Mull, Stephen, Michael Vickers, and Michael Hess. *Counterinsurgency for US Government Policy Makers: A Work in Progress.* Department of State Publication 11456: Bureau of Political-Military Affairs. Washington DC: 2007. http://www.usgcoin.org/library/USGDocuments/InterimCounterinsurgencyGuide(Oct2007).pdf (accessed November 15, 2007).

National Counter Terrorism Center. "National Strategy to Combat Terrorist Travel." May 2, 2006. http://www.nctc.gov/docs/u_terrorist_travel_book_may2_2006.pdf13 (accessed on December 16, 2007).

Office of Joint Chiefs of Staff. *JP 1-02 Dictionary of Military and Associated Terms.* Washington DC: Chairman Joint Chiefs of Staff 2001).

Office of Joint Chiefs of Staff. *JP 3-0 Joint Operations.* Washington DC: Chairman Joint Chiefs of Staff 2006.

Organization for Economic Co-operation and Development. "Ten years of combating money laundering." *OECD Observer* October 1999. http://www.oecdobserver.org/news/fullstory.php?aid=63 (accessed November 19, 2007).

People's Republic of China. "Chapter VII: Border and Costal Defense." China Internet Information Center. http://www.china.org.cn/english/features/book/194476.htm (accessed on Dec 19, 2007).

Piombo, Jessica. "Terrorism and US Counter-Terrorism Programs in Africa: An Overview." *Strategic Insights* Vol. VI, Issue 1. US Naval Postgraduate School: January 2007. http://www.ccc.nps.navy.mil/si/2007/Jan/piomboJan07.asp (accessed on Dec 17, 2007).

Smith, Hugh. "Terrorism in the Iguaza Falls Region: $100 Bills, A DIME at a Time." School of Advanced Military Studies 2005. Fort Leavenworth, KS: United States Army Command and General Staff College.

Smith, Sam. "U.S trains Djiboutian troops in border security." CJTF HOA press release, May 4, 2006. http://djibouti.usembassy.gov/u.s_trains_djiboutian_troops_in_border_security_may_04_2006 (accessed on Dec 17, 2007).

Stacy, William E. *US Army Border Operations in Germany: 1945-1983.* Germany: Military History Office, US Army Europe, 1984.

Stone, David. "Israeli Women Play Major Role in Israel Homeland Defense." *Women & Guns* July 2002. http://www.womenandguns.com/archive/old0702issue/israel0702.html (accessed on Dec 19, 2007).

Sub Committee on Investigations of House Committee on Homeland Security. "A Line in the Sand: Confronting the Threat at the Southwest Border." http://www.house.gov/mccaul/pdf/Investigaions-Border-Report.pdf (accessed on Dec 15, 2007).

Thurer, Daniel. "The 'failed State' and international law." *International Review of the Red Cross* No. 836 Dec. 31, 1999. http://www.icrc.org/web/eng/siteeng0.nsf/html/57JQ6U (accessed on Nov 17, 2007).

United Nations General Assembly. "Global Counter-Terrorism Strategy." New York: September 8, 2006. http://www.un.org/terrorism/index.shtml (accessed November 11, 2007).

U.S. Congress. Senate. Committee on Armed Services. *Nomination hearing for LTG David H. Petraeus to be General, and Commander Multi-National Force Iraq.* 110th Cong., 1st sess., January 23, 2007. http://armed-services.senate.gov/statemnt/2007/January/Petraeus%2001-23-07.pdf (accessed November 3, 2007).

U.S. Customs and Border Protection Agency. "BORTAC: defusing the hot spots." *Customs and Border Protection Today* May 2004. http://www.cbp.gov/xp/CustomsToday/2004/May/bortac.xml (accessed on Dec 31, 2007).

U.S. Customs and Border Protection Agency. "Strategic Plan 2005-2011." http://www.cbp.gov/linkhandler/cgov/toolbox/about/mission/strategic_plan_05_11.ctt/str ategic_plan_05_11.pdf (accessed on Nov 19, 2007).

U.S. Department of the Army. *FM 3-24 Counterinsurgency.* Washington D.C.: Department of the Army, 15 December 2006, Chap. 2.

U.S. Department of the Army. *FM 31-55 Border Security and Anti-Infiltration Operations.* Washington DC: Department of the Army, March 1972.

U.S. Department of State, "FY 2006 Performance and Accountability Highlights." http://www.state.gov/s/d/rm/rls/perfrpt/2006hlts/html/79818.htm (accessed November 4, 2007).

U.S. Department of State. "Israel and the Occupied territories." Bureau of Democracy, Human Rights and Labor Country Report on Human Rights 2006. http://www.state.gov/g/drl/rls/hrrpt/2006/78854.htm (accessed on Dec 20, 2007).

U.S. Department of State. *Trafficking in Persons Report.* June 2007. http://www.state.gov/documents/organization/82902.pdf (accessed on December 17, 2007).

Williams, Phil. "Combating Transnational Organized Crime." in *Transnational Threats: Blending Law Enforcement and Military Strategies.* Edited by Carolyn Pumphrey, 185-202. Carlisle, PA: Strategic Studies Institute, 2000.

Williams, Phil and Ernesto U. Savona, eds. *The United Nations and Transnational Crime.* London: Frank Cass &Co, 1996.

World Bank Group. Curbing the Epidemic: Governments and the Economics of Tobacco Control. Washington, 1999. http://www1.worldbank.org/tobacco/reports_pdf.asp (accessed December 2, 2007).

www.ingramcontent.com/pod-product-compliance
Lightning Source LLC
Chambersburg PA
CBHW082152290526

45794CB00008B/3269